How to Save Money

89 Saving Money Made Easy Tips

By: Miranda Grey

I0500268

TABLE OF CONTENTS

Publishers Notes...7

Disclaimer 8

Dedication 9

Introduction 10

Holiday Gift Giving...11

Clearance 12

Thrift/Surplus Stores 13

Thrift/Surplus Stores 13

Reuse 14

Landscaping..15

Budget..16

Plan 17

Buy in Bulk...18

Allowance 19

Insurance 20

Coupons...21

Credit Cards 22

Mortgage Payment...23

Credit Card Interest..24

Miranda Grey

Patience 25

Financial Consulting 26

Break old Habits 27

Avoid Temptations 28

The Right Time to Shop 29

Matinee 30

Make your Own Gifts 31

Barter System 32

Comparison Shop 33

Stop Competing with the Jones' 34

Sales Clerk Compliments 35

Incentives – Reward Plan 36

Dollar Stores 37

Don't Give up the Good Stuff 38

Utilities 39

Check the Garbage 40

Unsecured Creditors 41

Off-Season 42

Buy versus Rent or Lease 43

Buffet Meals 44

Cable Networking 45

Proper Maintenance 46

Company Stock / 401K 47

Family Haircuts 48

Wants versus Needs 49

Go Generic 50

Refinance 51

Stock Up 52

Shopping for Clothes...53

Carpool 54

Trendy Fashion 55

Free Entertainment 56

Telephone / Mobile Phone...57

Home Remedies 58

Pay on Time 59

Insulation..60

Cancel Subscriptions...61

Consolidate your Errands..62

Sell your Stuff...63

Turn your Hobby into Money.......................................64

Recycle 65

Heating and Cooling 66

Shop Online..67

Consignment Shops..68

Stay out of the Malls 69

Car Shopping 70

Check Receipts and Statements 71

Overdraft Protection 72

Bank Accounts 73

Organization 74

Good Health 75

Automobile Care 76

Vacations 77

Borrowing Money 78

Repair versus Replace 79

Dining Out 80

Plan Menus 81

Coordinate Efforts 82

Computer Software 83

Life Satisfaction 84

Live Within your Means 85

Christmas Fund 86

Previously Viewed 87

Dinner Guests 88

Instant Messaging / Microphone 89

Long Distance Calling 90

Ball Games..91

Discount Books...92

Baby Food...93

Squelch the Smoking...94

Rebate Programs 95

Seasonal Buys 96

Pocket Change 97

Freebies..98

See your Successes (Final Thoughts)..99

About the Author...100

Miranda Grey
PUBLISHERS NOTES

Speedy Publishing LLC

40 E. Main St., #1156

Newark, DE 19711

www.speedypublishing.co

Cover Artwork: 24 Hr. Designs Ltd.

Editing: Speedy Publishing LLC

Book design: Speedy Publishing LLC

ISBN:

This is a reprint book.

DISCLAIMER

This publication is intended to provide helpful and informative material. It is not intended to diagnose, treat, cure, or prevent any health problem or condition, nor is intended to replace the advice of a physician. No action should be taken solely on the contents of this book. Always consult your physician or qualified health-care professional on any matters regarding your health and before adopting any suggestions in this book or drawing inferences from it.

The author and publisher specifically disclaim all responsibility for any liability, loss or risk, personal or otherwise, which is incurred as a consequence, directly or indirectly, from the use or application of any contents of this book.

Any and all product names referenced within this book are the trademarks of their respective owners. None of these owners have sponsored, authorized, endorsed, or approved this book.

Always read all information provided by the manufacturers' product labels before using their products. The author and publisher are not responsible for claims made by manufacturers.

Miranda Grey

DEDICATION

This book is dedicated to my colleague and mentor Mindy.

INTRODUCTION

People are always trying to save money, especially with today's economy. No matter what your reason for saving, through this e-book, you will discover ways never considered.

The price of everything has gone up, requiring people to be more conscientious about money. The problem is that by the time the mortgage, car, utilities, and credit cards are paid, there is little money to put aside. Saving money is not that hard, just a matter of learning all the different options and being creative.

In addition to the obvious of putting money into a retirement fund or savings account, there are hundreds of ways to save money. Although some ways of saving may not seem like much, once you add them up at the end of the year, you will see how substantial the savings really are. Keep in mind that saving is more than a single lump sum of money put aside. Saving is something found in your everyday life by the way you live and the choices you make.

Rome was not built in a day and neither will your bank account be. Each penny saved is one more penny than before. If you have the ability to save big, that is great. However, most people are not in that position, which is why this course will show you how little savings can add up quickly.

Be encouraged that it is never too late to start saving, regardless of your age. Set your mind that now is the time to start building your future.

I'll be sharing 89 simple and creative tips to get you on the right path.

Miranda Grey

HOLIDAY GIFT GIVING

This tip is especially helpful for large families. Although it is fun buying for and receiving from everyone, it can be very expensive. Make an agreement with your family that you will continue to buy for the children but that the adults will go with a name exchange. This way the children are not disappointed and you can spend a little more on one or two people rather than spreading your money thin. For the members that you did not pick to exchange with, bake a loaf of their favorite homemade bread or cookies.

CLEARANCE

Always head straight for the clearance rack where you can find amazing bargains. Sometimes you may have to dig a little to find the right item but the savings will be well-worth your time. Most clearance racks offer variety, current trends, and great value. For example, Bed, Bath & Beyond has a clearance section where you can find all kinds of wonderful household items for a fraction of the original cost.

Miranda Grey
THRIFT/SURPLUS STORES

Unfortunately, thrift and surplus stores have been given a bad rap. Many of these stores are filled with hundreds of top quality items. Name brand merchandise is easy to find but just like clearance racks, it takes some time to find. Find a thrift or surplus store close to where you live and then plan spending some time to find those outstanding bargains. One woman in Kansas City, Missouri located such a store about 20 minutes from her home.

After shopping through every isle over the period of two hours, she walked out of the store with eight huge garbage bags filled to the brim with designer clothes for her and her children, many with the original tags still attached. She even found a couple of Liz Claiborne suits for herself at $5.99 each and a Dooney & Burke purse normally valued at $225 for $19.95. Her children had an entire season of school clothes and best of all, she paid less than $200.

REUSE

When you shop, look for items that can be reused. Rechargeable batteries are a perfect example. Even though the initial purchase may be more than non-rechargeable batteries, there is a definite savings over a long period. Another option would be to purchase a nice artificial Christmas tree. Many of the current artificial trees look amazingly real and with the right lights and ornaments, you can change the look from year to year.

Miranda Grey

LANDSCAPING

If you are considering creating a nice flower garden area, shopping for plants even on sale, can be expensive. Before you go out and start spending, look around to see if you have other plants that can be split from your existing flowers. Additionally, if you have a good relationship with any of your neighbors, you might ask them if they have any plants you could use as a starter. Another great idea is the next time you are in the market to buy a lawnmower, purchase one that mulches leaves. This way, rather than buy mulch for your flowerbeds every year, you can simply use the mulch you make.

BUDGET

Everyone should create a budget. If you are not sure how or just not good with money, many businesses such as H&R Block, offer free financial consulting to help you put a budget together. Knowing where you are spending your money is by far the best way to save. In most cases, people have no idea where their money is really going and once they see it on paper, not only are they surprised but eager to change their spending habits.

Miranda Grey

PLAN

Planning is a great way to save. Before you go to the grocery store, make a list and stick with it. If considering a vacation, plan everything. Heading out with no set direction will certainly lead you to impulsive spending.

BUY IN BULK

It is true that warehouse shopping can save a lot of money. Even if you have a small family, you can always split large quantities. The price of items in bulk is generally a great bargain. If you are single, you might go in with friends or family on bulk items.

Miranda Grey

ALLOWANCE

Do not forget to give yourself an allowance for things you enjoy. Even if on a tight budget, buy something that you enjoy, which could be as simple as buying a new shirt or grabbing lunch at your favorite café. If you do not allow yourself this small "splurge", you could find yourself in the same position as if dieting. Total deprivation leads to overindulgence.

INSURANCE

Shop around for insurance and work with a good agent that can provide information on discounts such as good student, multi-car discount, etc. Some people think the price of insurance is the same from one company to the next. However, prices can vary dramatically and to ensure you get the best deal, you need to consider all your options

Miranda Grey

Coupons

Okay, maybe you used to laugh as you watched people pull out their coupons at stores but the truth is that using coupons can save you hundreds of dollars every year. Coupons can be used at grocery stores, retail chains, any store where the item is sold. Some stores offer double coupon days, which is an extra bonus. On average, you could easily save from 5% to 15% on a bill for $100 simply by presenting a coupon. Coupons are not just for food items and by scouring your local newspaper you can find coupons for all sorts of merchandise.

CREDIT CARDS

Use credit cards only for emergency. Although convenient, credit cards are dangerous and damaging. In addition, if you have a credit card that has a $1,000 balance and you pay only the minimum payment each month, it will take you between 20 and 30 years to pay off that $1,000 balance since the majority of money is going strictly toward the interest and not the principal amount.

Miranda Grey

Mortgage Payment

Paying one additional mortgage payment each year, whether in a lump sum or monthly increments, can lower a 30-year loan down to 18 years. If you pay more than one extra payment, the number of years will decrease even more. Since this additional payment will be applied only to the principal and not the interest, you end up saving thousands and thousands of dollars once the home is paid off.

CREDIT CARD INTEREST

If you have credit cards and your credit is in good standing, call your credit card company, and ask for your interest rate to be lowered. It is truly that simple. Unfortunately, most people do not even realize this is an option so they never make the call. Just tell the representative that you want a better rate on your credit card and they will take care of your request.

Miranda Grey

PATIENCE

Be patient when it comes to saving. This means that you need to accept that it will take time to save and good planning. Be patient and remember that just because you want something, do not rush to buy just to satisfy your urge. Instead, wait for sales in order to get the best price, which in turn will save you money.

FINANCIAL CONSULTING

Many financial companies and even churches offer outstanding classes on how to manage money. While some of these programs are free, others may have a nominal fee of around $35 to attend but the money is well spent. Another great option is consumer-counseling services. This is a great option for people in over their head with debt. The counselors will work directly with your creditors to lower your balances, interest rate, and establish workable payments that you can afford.

Miranda Grey

BREAK OLD HABITS

Take time to learn the various things that "trigger" your spending. When you are depressed, lonely, sad, anxious, excited, whatever it may be, do you spend more? Once you can identify these triggers then you can learn how to control them. As an example, if you were just laid off from your job, although money is tight, you may have an overwhelming "need" to spend money. Perhaps you notice that when you are bored, you head for the shops. Knowing what affects you will help you to discipline yourself to find other ways of comfort.

AVOID TEMPTATIONS

If you have a particular weakness, stay away from it. If you love to gamble, stay out of the casinos. If you have a weakness for shoes, drive past your favorite shoe store. While avoiding temptation is hard, it is also necessary in order to save money. When you want to give into your temptation, this is the time to use your "allowance".

Miranda Grey

THE RIGHT TIME TO SHOP

Studies have proven that when shopping while hungry, depressed, tired, and stressed, you buy more. Before you head to the grocery store, eat something. If you are upset or feeling a little blue, calm yourself down or wait until you feel better before you head out to shop. As funny as it may sound, having a clear mind is important when it comes to shopping and spending money.

MATINEE

Do you love the movies but hate the prices? Switch your nighttime show to the late afternoon or early evening matinee. The price is about 50% less and when taking an entire family, that is a nice savings. Pop your own popcorn, put in a plastic bag, and place in a large purse and make or buy your own candy, leaving only drinks to buy. Food at the theater is outrageously priced. The next time that you head to the movies, hit the matinee, stuff those jellybeans and licorice sticks in your purse, and enjoy the savings. Also, check for movie tickets online, which can be discounted.

Miranda Grey

Make your Own Gifts

If you ask people if they prefer a store bought or handmade gift, the majority would choose the latter. Handmade gifts are individualized and come from the heart. When you have a birthday, anniversary, baby shower, wedding, or Christmas gift to give, make the gift.

For Christmas, you could make a beautiful ornament or door wreath, for a baby shower you could purchase an inexpensive bib pattern and make special bibs, or for a wedding, you could create a wonderful album of photos showing the couples dating life. Other great options include making homemade hot chocolate, soaps, candles, or lotions and placing them in inexpensive glass containers or baskets purchased at a thrift shop. If you use a mason jar, add foam and fabric under the lid for added color, use a label to write the contents and a message of endearment, and wrap a nice piece of ribbon around the ridge. The options are endless, so get creative.

BARTER SYSTEM

Gather friends, family, neighbors, and co-workers and set up a bartering system. Offer babysitting to one family in exchange for them mowing your lawn or offer to clean someone's house in exchange for a week of car-pooling your child to school. You would be amazed at the opportunities and the money that can be saved using a bartering system.

Miranda Grey

COMPARISON SHOP

Comparison-shopping can make a big difference in the price you pay. You might be looking at a barbecue grill at one place for $350.00 and by making two more stops, find the exact grill or one comparable for $300. In addition, consider the price of items assembled versus unassembled. For example, you might find the barbecue grill unassembled for $250. A couple of hours of "fun" assembling the grill is certainly worth a $100 saving.

STOP COMPETING WITH THE JONES'

You do not have to compete with anyone. Be proud of what you have and who you are. If you can only afford an inexpensive sofa from a thrift store, find a nice throw, make a few pillows, and be proud and thankful. Competitiveness is a part of nature and to a degree, healthy. However, when competition creates a buying war to see who can have the "best" when they have no business buying at all, then it becomes damaging. Stick to what you can afford regardless of what anyone else has or pressure you might be feeling.

Miranda Grey

SALES CLERK COMPLIMENTS

Sales clerks are often paid on commission. Therefore, when you walk into a store and try on an expensive suit, you can be guaranteed you will hear several times over how wonderful you look, how great that suit fits you, etc. Because this is how the clerks make their money, they will say whatever it takes to make the sale. You probably do look good but do not allow yourself to be pressured into buying something beyond your means. Know what you want, the price range you can work with, and stick with your own rules, not theirs.

INCENTIVES – REWARD PLAN

To help you and your family spend more wisely, set up a system where rewards are given when the rules set forth are followed. For example, if a family decision was made to start making lunch and brown bagging it to work and school instead of paying each day, the incentive might be that if this is followed strictly for one month, the entire family can spend a Saturday at the Zoo or favorite theme park.

Miranda Grey

Dollar Stores

Many years ago, dollar stores offered only off brand products or poorly made merchandise. However, that has completely changed. Now you can walk into a dollar store and find the same name brand laundry soap, cleaning supplies, clothing, school supplies, everything for a fraction of the cost. Where a store name brand bottle of laundry detergent might cost $6.50 at a grocery store, you can find the identical product and size at the dollar store for $2.50. Check out your local dollar store and enjoy the mountains of savings.

DON'T GIVE UP THE GOOD STUFF

A misconception is that while trying to save money you have to deal with sub-par merchandise, which is untrue. If you love fresh breads and pastries, visit a bakery thrift store. For your fresh fruits and vegetables, visit your local farmer's market. Try eBay or other auction sites to buy top quality merchandise for a huge discount. Watch for neighborhood garage sales or estate sales and auctions to find items you need. Just because you are looking for bargains as a way of saving money does not mean you have to skimp on quality.

Miranda Grey

UTILITIES

Set up some rules in your home such as turning lights off when leaving the room, having only a parent adjust the air or heat, leaving the doors or windows open when letting either cold or hot air into the house. Utilities are expensive and a great money saver is to monitor how they are used in your home. Another great idea is the investment of buying an energy-efficient hot water heater. If you cannot afford one, lower the setting so you are not heating water so hot. The hotter the setting, the more energy used.

CHECK THE GARBAGE

One woman had her teenage daughter clean her room. The daughter proudly did just that, filling two huge trash bags of things she no longer wanted. Out of curiosity, the mother peeked into one of the bags to see what was being thrown away. In shock, she found a new tube of suntan lotion, two perfectly good sweaters, makeup, lotion, a picture frame, hair curlers, all good things. The daughter did not realize that just because the items were of no interest to her, they might be to someone else. After talking to her daughter, the mom turned around and listed the items on eBay, making a $35 profit on her daughter's "junk."

UNSECURED CREDITORS

Make a list of all your unsecured debts along with creditor contact information and payoff amount so you can have an accurate record of how much you owe. Choose one creditor, possibly a credit card, and focus on paying off that bill. Once you have achieved that goal, choose another. Start with the debt that has the highest interest rate since it is the one costing you the most money.

Off-Season

The next time you plan a vacation, consider off-season. Generally, the prices for airfare, hotel, and cars are substantially lower than traveling during peak time. If you look at all your options, you will find that in many cases, you can come close to the date you would like to travel. As an example, flying to Hawaii through June 8 is considered off-season while June 9 is peak. One day makes a huge difference in price.

Miranda Grey

BUY VERSUS RENT OR LEASE

When looking at homes or automobiles check the rent and lease options. Depending on your particular situation, renting or leasing may be a better financial decision. Weigh all your options and see which choice makes the best sense from a financial standpoint.

BUFFET MEALS

When taking the family out to dinner, consider restaurants that have buffets. In many cases, the prices are outstanding and a parent can share with a small child. In addition, many buffets are "all you can eat" and of course, there is something for everyone.

Miranda Grey

Cable Networking

If you have a computer upstairs and another downstairs and you use high-speed data, have one of the computers be the primary computer and the other be the backup. This way, you are only charged once for Internet access and a small fee of $10 to $15 a month for the second computer. This is a great bargain!

PROPER MAINTENANCE

Purchase an annual home warranty policy. These policies can run from $350 to $500 a year and offer extremely valuable options. The way most of these policies work is that if you have something break, such as your garage door, dishwasher, air conditioner, etc., for a minimal fee, usually $50 to $100, a serviceperson will come to your home to fix the item. Best of all, if you have five things broken and the same serviceperson is qualified to fix all of them, you are still charged the $50 to $100 fee once, not five times. For your automobile, you might look into purchasing an extended warranty. If you ever need either one of these policies, they will save you tremendous value.

COMPANY STOCK / 401K

Contributing to employee stock options or a 401K plan is a wonderful opportunity to save. Most companies will match your contribution, sometimes dollar for dollar, up to a maximum, generally 6%. From each paycheck, you can have a small amount of money deducted (1%) and up. Over time, that money grows and since the business is providing a match, you get free money.

FAMILY HAIRCUTS

Look for hair styling shops that offer family deals or learn how to cut hair yourself. Many families take care of their own haircuts and put the money they would have spent aside as a vacation fund. This system works out perfectly.

Miranda Grey

WANTS VERSUS NEEDS

Make sure the thing you want to spend your money on is a "need" and not a "want." Sometimes this can seem like a fine gray line but if you stick to the need list, you will spend less.

GO GENERIC

When buying food, try some of the generic items. Unless you or your guests are connoisseurs of fine dining, they will not know if the green beans were generic or a top name brand. Once you add some butter, salt, and pepper, no one will know the difference except you - $79 per can versus $33 per can! People do not realize that many generic brands are actually manufactured by name brand companies, just branded with a different name. In fact, companies such as those that make snack foods will have conveyor belts that run side-by-side – one for the name brand and one for the generic brand. This is quite common and the only difference is the label and price.

Miranda Grey

REFINANCE

With interest rates being so low, consider refinancing your home and/or securing a debt consolidation loan. You might have to come up with a new closing cost but once paid, you will have lower payments, better terms, and save thousands of dollars over the years.

STOCK UP

As you shop, if you notice that a brand you and your family use on a consistent basis is on sale for a great bargain, stock up. As an example, if you use a particular type of shampoo costing $4.50 per bottle and you find it on sale for $2.50, go ahead and buy two bottles. You should only do this on items you know will be used.

Miranda Grey

SHOPPING FOR CLOTHES

There are many secrets relating to saving money on clothing. As a perfect example, rather than buy a matched suit for $450, buy the pieces separate. This will save you about $100 to $150. Additionally, buy several pieces that can be mixed and matched, giving you six outfits out of four pieces.

CARPOOL

In some larger cities, carpooling is required in order to reduce smog. However, regardless of where you live, carpooling can also be a big money saver. Check with co-workers and determine who lives close enough to share a ride. By the end of the year, you will have saved several hundreds of dollars.

Miranda Grey

TRENDY FASHION

Most people love to dress in the most up-to-date fashion but for those fashions, you pay big bucks. Consider dressing with basics and then emphasis them with trendy accessories. This will save you money on the clothing that is less expensive while allowing you to dress it up.

FREE ENTERTAINMENT

If you are tired of being bored, you will be pleased to learn that there are hundreds of things to do that do not cost a dime. For example, if you want a little Friday or Saturday night excitement, sign up at your local police department for a "ride-a-long" where you can go on duty with an officer as they respond to real calls.

Community colleges are always offering free exercise classes, or coffee shops have poetry readings. Entertainment and having fun does not have to cost anything. Some cities have special areas that are popular on the weekends where you can find free concerts. Check your local paper and college to get a list for your area.

Miranda Grey

Telephone / Mobile Phone

First, shop around for the best deals. Second, stay away from all the fun bells and whistles and just stick with the basic plan. Some people have turned to shutting down their home telephone and are now using their mobile phones in place. Since most wireless carriers offer free long-distance, call waiting, call forwarding, caller ID, voicemail, and more, it can do the same as a regular phone but for less. Why have two phones when you can have just one?

HOME REMEDIES

Before rushing off to see the doctor for a sore throat, try some home remedies or over the counter drugs instead. For a sore throat, butter mixed with ginger and sugar makes a soothing healing pate. A hot toddy before bed is great for a cold. Simply ask your family for their home remedies and try it. Sometimes a simple over the counter medication or herb will do the trick without costing you an expensive doctor's office visit.

PAY ON TIME

For every payment you pay late, you are charged a late fee, which can range from $25 to $50 or more depending on the company. Therefore, if you just made a $50 payment but it was paid late, nothing was paid toward the debt. Instead, the entire $50 went toward an unnecessary fee. To avoid spending unnecessary money, be sure you mail your check in time to avoid these fees.

INSULATION

Hundreds of dollars are wasted every year from the average home due to improper insulation. Make sure there are no drafts coming from your window, door, or fireplace. Ensure your home has the appropriate level of insulation, which will make a HUGE difference in your utility bill.

Miranda Grey

Cancel Subscriptions

It is always fun getting your favorite magazine or book in the mail but you should cancel them or at least most of them. If you have several subscriptions, choose one or two to keep and cancel the rest.

CONSOLIDATE YOUR ERRANDS

To save gas, organize your day of errands so you get as much done in an organized manner as possible. Stay in the same geographical area and hit as many of your errands in that area as possible to avoid excessive driving.

Miranda Grey

Sell your Stuff

Go through your house and pull together all the items you no longer use. These can include small or large appliances, gardening tools, clothing, makeup, and sporting equipment, whatever you have, and then list them on eBay.com or Halfoff.com. Take the money earned from these sales and put it in your savings account not to be touched.

TURN YOUR HOBBY INTO MONEY

Everyone has a skill – find yours and turn it into money. For example, if you have a skill for woodworking, start creating children's toys, or curio cabinets to sell. Perhaps you are computer savvy and could teach a class at your local community college. Find something you enjoy and sell it.

RECYCLE

Try a different type of recycling that will save you money. Have you ever received a nice gift that you like from someone but will never use? Rather than take it back to the store for an exchange, consider keeping it to give as a gift to someone else. Another way to recycle is to look around your home. There are always things right in your home that can be used to make nice gift baskets – things you never use. For example, the next time you purchase shower gel where you buy one and get one free, keep one for yourself and set the other one aside for future gift giving. You will find hundreds of ideas so be creative and consider things you purchased but have never used.

HEATING AND COOLING

Make sure vents in rooms not being used or the garage are closed. Many people tend to try to heat and cool the entire home. Instead, take the time to close off areas that you are not using. You will save substantial money on your utilities.

Miranda Grey

SHOP ONLINE

Many online businesses offer great bargains and in some cases, free shipping. Since the Internet is such a competitive market, you can usually find fantastic deals. In addition, many of your favorite businesses where you shop in person have websites that offer even greater savings. Bookstores such as Amazon.com will sell books up to 70% off the original price. Overstock.com is another online business that sells closeout items for fantastic bargains.

CONSIGNMENT SHOPS

Rather than throw out or sell slightly worn clothing or other household items in a garage sale, consider selling them through a consignment shop. You will get a better price for your items and consignment shops are always looking for quality merchandise. Check out Half.com, which is an online consignment shop offering books, movies, computer software, and much more in either new or used condition.

Miranda Grey

STAY OUT OF THE MALLS

If possible, stay away from shopping malls. High-dollar shopping malls have expensive overhead and are designed to sell, sell, sell. Prices are generally higher and in most cases, people walk out with more than they anticipated buying. It is better to shop at stand-alone shops or on the Internet.

CAR SHOPPING

Shop around for the best price. While you may have your eye on that "perfect" car and want it now, by waiting and looking around, you could be saving yourself a lot of money. In addition, check out other states. If you live within a few hours' drive from other cities, check out the price difference. The five hours it takes to drive may be worth the money saved.

Miranda Grey

CHECK RECEIPTS AND STATEMENTS

If you were to check your grocery or store receipt, approximately 50% of the time you would find an overcharge. This happens all the time and in some cases, the charge can be substantial. The same is true for credit card statements, bank statements, phone bills, etc. Check the detail because it is quite common to find errors. These mistakes can easily be corrected simply by asking and providing a copy of the receipt or statement.

OVERDRAFT PROTECTION

Almost everyone has at one point or another had an insufficient check. Most banks charge $20 per returned check, which if not careful with your account, can quickly add up to a lot of money. If you have a savings account, consider adding overdraft protection onto your checking account so if you ever go into a negative balance, the money would automatically be covered by your savings. Most banks offer this service free.

Bank Accounts

Make sure you work with a qualified banker that can set up the "right" kind of account for your type of spending. There are numerous options specifically designed for people that write a good number of checks versus those who do not. Check with your existing bank to ensure you have what you really need and if they are not willing to work with you, change banks. In general, credit unions are good options. Their rates are typically lower and because they are employee owned, you can find better options.

ORGANIZATION

You may be wondering what being organized has to do with saving money but in reality, it has a lot to do with it. For example, if you miss a credit card due date by one day, you will be charged anywhere from a 15% to 25% penalty. The same would be true for taxes. Missing one simple date can cost thousands. You need to be organized so you know the exact dates your bills are due as well as keep all receipts, contracts, etc. in an orderly manner.

Miranda Grey

GOOD HEALTH

You need to make sure you take care of yourself physically. Missed dental cleanings (every six months) can lead to gum disease or tooth decay that can cost thousands to fix. The same is true for your health. After trying home remedies or over the counter medications, if you still do not feel well, see a doctor. It is far better to pay the doctor visit than to let your simple summer cold turn into pneumonia.

Automobile Care

Keep your car oil changed, tires rotated, and overall care up-to-date. First, the $30 for your oil change will save wear and tear on your car, which could result in significant money. Second, you need your car to get to and from work. By not having your car in top working condition could put you in a bad position when it comes to required transportation.

Miranda Grey

VACATIONS

While Paris, England, or Germany offers excitement, they also cost money to visit. Unfortunately, people on a regular basis forget about the United States and even the very state in which they live. One man had lived in Arizona his entire life. At age 50, when asked by a friend what the Grand Canyon was like, he was unable to answer because he had never been there. The next time you get ready to plan your family vacation, look around where you live and consider an exciting road trip that will not only be educating but cost effective. A vacation does not have to be expensive to be fun and memorable.

BORROWING MONEY

Unless you have an emergency, avoid those enticing advertisements to lend you money at incredible rates. Banks and lending institutions make it much too easy to borrow money and especially during the holidays, they flash all their great advertisements drawing people in. Afterwards, you have borrowed money that you could have done without and now you are locked into a five-year repayment contract. If you want a new car or boat, it is better to save. If you do need a new car, avoid brand new cars, which lose massive amounts of appreciation the minute you drive off the lot. Instead, look for something a year or two old where you will still have a nice car but much more in line with an appropriate cost.

Miranda Grey

REPAIR VERSUS REPLACE

Instead of spending $1,000 on that beautiful new couch, you might consider one of two options. If your couch frame is still good, you might spend $300 to have it recovered or purchase a quality slipcover for $100. Your couch will look brand new for much less, than it would to replace. Another example would be if you have a lamp that you want to replace. Consider painting it and adding a new shade rather than spending money to buy a brand new one. Perhaps you have a washer, dryer, or refrigerator that is running a little sluggish. Find out the cost of repair over that of purchasing a new one. Even if you have an appliance with the wrong color, businesses offer fantastic paint jobs. With a little creativity, you will be amazed at how much can be repaired, thus saving you money.

DINING OUT

Eating out can be expensive. Rather than stop eating out, simply cut back and look for options of two-for-one. Restaurants of all calibers offer weekly specials and if you check in your Sunday paper, you can often find special bargains. You might even think about signing up as a Mystery Shopper on the Internet where you can eat at fine restaurants free or at a huge discount just for writing a report on the food, service, and cleanliness.

Miranda Grey

Plan Menus

Although it will take some time initially, after you have planned a week's menu once, it will become much easier and best of all, it will save you money. Knowing exactly what you will be making helps you to shop for foods that can be used more than once. As an example, if you are going to have spaghetti on Tuesday, you could buy bulk ground beef at a better price and then use the other half for tacos on Saturday. Another option would be buying round steak where one night you fix Salisbury steak and then a few days later, you use the leftovers for breakfast hash. This will help you stretch meals and avoid last minute or impulse buying.

COORDINATE EFFORTS

If you are married, make sure you and your spouse are working on the same agenda. If one is trying to save money while the other is busy spending, what is the point? When you work as a team, you can encourage each other to keep on track with your saving.

Miranda Grey

COMPUTER SOFTWARE

In order to keep on track with your debts and credits, you need to use some type of software such as Quicken or Quick Books. This will keep you focused on your goals and tasks while you strive to achieve them. Additionally, rather than buy software programs to download, first check Download.com or Freeware.com to see if there are free versions to download.

LIFE SATISFACTION

Learn how to enjoy life and nature rather than possessions. The next time you feel like spending money, head to your local park where you can enjoy the warm sun, green grass, and towering trees without spending a dime. Being happy in life is far better than buying item after item. Having an inner peace is better than having a house filled with "things." That does not mean you cannot enjoy some of the finer things in life it just means learning how to be happy with yourself and not "things."

Miranda Grey

LIVE WITHIN YOUR MEANS

The quickest way to get in debt is to live beyond your means. Sure, most people want more than they have but life is not all about spending money. Be thankful for what you do have and learn how to enjoy the financial position you are in. This is where your budget will help identify the amount of money coming in against the amount of debt going out.

CHRISTMAS FUND

Many banks and financial institutions offer a Christmas Fund program. This is an excellent way to put aside some money for your holiday shopping so you do not end up with a ton of spending. With these programs, you do not even miss the money and better yet, less stress around the holidays.

Miranda Grey

Previously Viewed

Home videos and DVDs are hot items and perfect for any family entertainment. Now you can visit the major video chains and purchase previously viewed videos and DVDs for about half the cost. For example, at Blockbuster, you can purchase either one and get a 30-day warranty. This is still a wonderful way to have quality entertainment for a terrific savings. Another great option is to record your own movies either from TV or any of the popular cable channels such as HBO, Showtime or Disney. Rather than hitting the theater every weekend, make it a special occasion. Instead, pop your popcorn, grab a soda, spread out a blanket, and create your own theater-type atmosphere.

DINNER GUESTS

Invite friends over for dinner as a potluck. People love sharing their favorite recipe and by splitting dinner, everyone enjoys variety while saving money. In fact, make this a tradition amongst your friends.

Instant Messaging / Microphone

Rather than spend a small fortune in long distance, contact friends and family via instant messaging on the Internet. In addition, you can download a program that will allow you to connect a microphone and actually have a voice conversation free. All you pay for is the normal price of your Internet connection, which generally runs from $9.95 to $21.95 a month. Either option allows you to have real-time conversations for no extra money.

LONG DISTANCE CALLING

If you do plan to use long-distance calling, shop around for the right carrier and be sure to read the small print. Even if you like your current carrier, you might be able to find an equally liked carrier for less money. Long distance is a very competitive market so deals are easy to find. The same would be true for your wireless carrier. The plans range vastly from one carrier to another so check out all your options for the best one. Do not forget to look at the coverage area. If you choose a carrier that does not have the right coverage for your area, even if the price is better, there is no savings if you cannot send or receive calls.

Miranda Grey

BALL GAMES

Instead of spending your money on overpriced items at the ballgame, take your own cooler of food. Some professional stadiums no longer allow this so check before going. If you have a son or daughter that plays little league or soccer, this is a great way to save money over paying high concession stand prices.

DISCOUNT BOOKS

Purchase a discount coupon book, which generally costs around $25. As long as you use it faithfully and base your choices on options featured in the book, you can save hundreds of dollars. These books are great for restaurants, hotels, car rentals, and tons of entertainment and provide great variety and even better discounts.

Miranda Grey

BABY FOOD

Instead of buying expensive baby food, make your own. You can use fresh vegetables such as peas, green beans, or corn, run it through the blender, and then freeze individual servings in ice cube trays. When it comes time to feed the baby, simply pop out a cube of food, defrost, and you have instant food. This is a real time and money saver. Most foods can be frozen. In fact, if you make family foods like spaghetti or soups simply make a smaller portion with less salt and spice, puree, freeze just like the vegetables.

SQUELCH THE SMOKING

This is probably the hardest habit to break but in addition to saving your health, you will also save money. Cigarettes have become quite expensive and if you can quit smoking, you will enjoy breathing easier and having more to put away for a rainy day.

Miranda Grey

REBATE PROGRAMS

When you shop, always keep your eyes open for rebate programs. Although filling out the forms and clipping the UPC codes from a box is a hassle, the money you save is worth it. Some rebate items are not listed as offering a rebate. Check out AsmartShop.com or Rebateplace.com to see if any of your recent purchases offer a rebate.

Seasonal Buys

One to three days after a holiday, stores mark their holiday items from 50% to 75% off. This is an ideal way to stock up on next year's Christmas or Halloween decorations. This is true for stores that sell seasonal clothing as well. Shopping for jackets or sweaters in the summer will provide you with great deals.

Miranda Grey

Pocket Change

Keep a jar or some type of container handy and each time you come home, drop in your change. Every time you break a bill, put the change in your container. You will be amazed how quickly your money will build.

FREEBIES

Check out freebie sites such as TotallyFreebies.com or SassySue.com where you will find all types of sample items ranging from cosmetics to books to clothing. Most have no shipping charges and the ones that do are minimal. By filling out a few forms, you will receive sample size soaps, lotions, shampoos and conditioners, etc., which are ideal for the traveler.

SEE YOUR SUCCESSES (FINAL THOUGHTS)

It is important to have an understanding of money. Keep a journal where you can see your successes when it comes to saving money. This is a difficult task and takes time to learn but worth it. By keeping a list of the situations or ways you have saved money in front of you, you will be encouraged to keep going. These successes can be small or large. For example, if you normally buy your lunch, costing you from $5.00 to $7.00 per day and one week straight you packed your own lunch for $3.00 per day that is a success. If you wanted to buy a new dress but held off until it went on sale, saving 50%, that is another success.

Thank you for taking time to take my course, "89 Little Known Secrets To Saving Money.."!

ABOUT THE AUTHOR

Miranda learned to avoid shopping as an extreme emotional outlet. Many of us are guilty of spending when we are stressed, bored or depressed. Yes, no one can deny that shopping gives us momentary satisfaction and happiness. This perk-me-up feeling will wane as the novelty wears off. One way to avoid shopping during times when there is an extreme emotional surge is to enjoy the simple pleasures in life such as catching up with a friend over a cup of coffee, cooking a new dish for the family or having a picnic in the park. In her book she looks on things like how to buy time.

Buying time is essential and effective strategy to avoid impulsive shopping. I shamefully admit that I tend to surf the net from time to time for luxury items like accessories. From experience, I've learnt that impulsive shopping will lead to regret. Once the novelty of the item wears off, I realize that I don't really need the item as it is never or rarely used. Buying time helps to put my spending in check as it gives me time to rationalize and weigh out the pros and cons of the item I have been eyeing.

Grab a copy of How to Save Money Today!

www.ingramcontent.com/pod-product-compliance
Lightning Source LLC
Chambersburg PA
CBHW071237170526
45165CB00003B/1139